Henri Lazarof

TEXTURES

For Piano and 5 Instrumental Groups

Associated Music Publishers, Inc.

DISTRIBUTED BY

HAL•LEONARD®

7777 W. BLUEMOUND RD. P.O. BOX 13819 MILWAUKEE, WI 53213

Dedicated to David Atherton and John Ogdon

Note

Henri Lazarof's *Textures* — commissioned by the London Sinfonietta — was first performed at Queen Elizabeth Hall, London, on January 13, 1971. John Ogdon was the soloist with the London Sinfonietta, David Atherton conducting.

COMPLETE INSTRUMENTATION

Solo Piano
Flute
Alto Flute
Oboe
English Horn
Bb Clarinet
Bass Clarinet

2 F Horns
2 Bb Trumpets
2 Trombones
   (1 tenor, 1 bass)
Tuba

Violin I ⎤
Violin II ⎥
Viola   ⎬ *soli*
Cello   ⎥
Bass   ⎦
Harp
Celesta and Harmonium

Percussion
(4 players)

2 Chime Sets
Glockenspiel
2 Vibraphones
2 Xylophones
4 Timpani

2 Snare Drums
2 Tenor Drums
3 Tom-Toms
Bass Drum

5 Temple Blocks
2 Suspended Cymbals
   (medium, large)
2 Tam-Tams
   (medium, large)

Duration: ca. 23:30

Orchestra material available on rental from the publisher.

Performance Notes

In the score, the following indications are referred to by their corresponding number:

1. Accidentals apply only to the notes they precede and to their immediate repetition at the exact pitch.
2. ♩ = plucked string.
3. ♩ = stopped note on the string with the l.h.
4. ╱ = slowly come back to a naturally struck note.
5. Lightly brush the strings once between approximate pitches.
6. Hit strings with fingers of the l.h.
7. With two palms on the lowest part of the keyboard.
8. N.C. = no conducting.
9. All instruments sound as written.

DISTRIBUTION OF INSTRUMENTS

Group I
Flute
Oboe
Bb Clarinet
Violin I (*solo*)
Viola (*solo*)

Group II
Bb Trumpet 1
Tenor Trombone

{ Chimes
Vibraphone
Snare Drum
Tenor Drum
3 Tom-Toms
Suspended Cymbal (*medium*)
Tam-Tam (*medium*) }

{ Glockenspiel
Xylophone
2 Timpani }

Group III
Alto Flute
English Horn
Bass Clarinet
Violin II (*solo*)
Cello (*solo*)

Group IV
Bb Trumpet 2
Bass Trombone

{ Chimes
Vibraphone
Snare Drum
Tenor Drum
Bass Drum
5 Temple Blocks
Suspended Cymbal (*large*)
Tam-Tam (*large*) }

{ Xylophone
2 Timpani }

Group V
F Horn 1
F Horn 2
Tuba
Bass (*solo*)

Harp

Celesta-Harmonium
(*one player*)

Solo Piano

iv

SEATING DIAGRAM

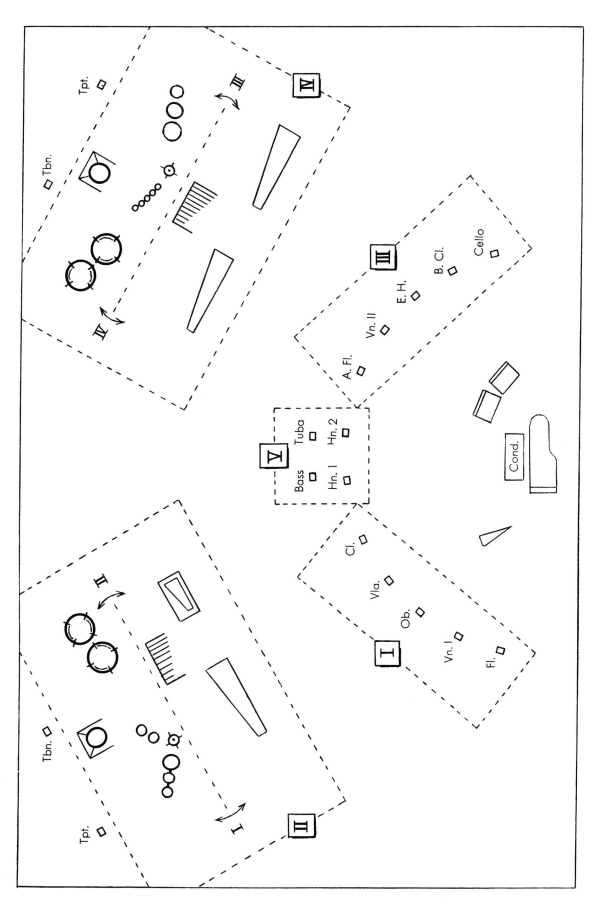

TEXTURES
for Piano and 5 Instrumental Groups

Henri Lazarof

4

8

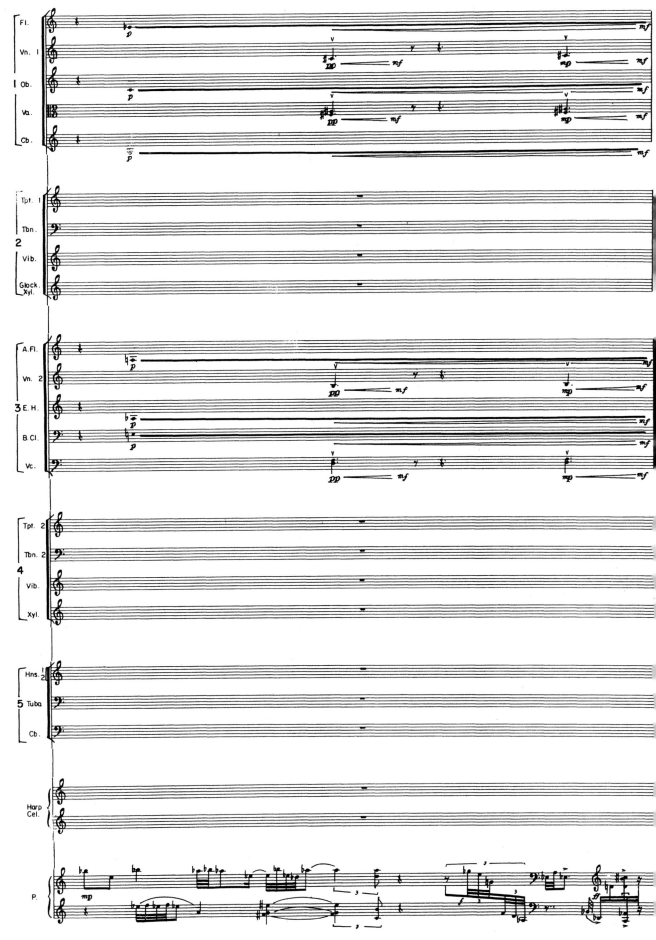

12

14

repeat in any order until

1) These 4 figures can be repeated in any order and frequency.

1) Conduct in 3
2) Conduct in 6

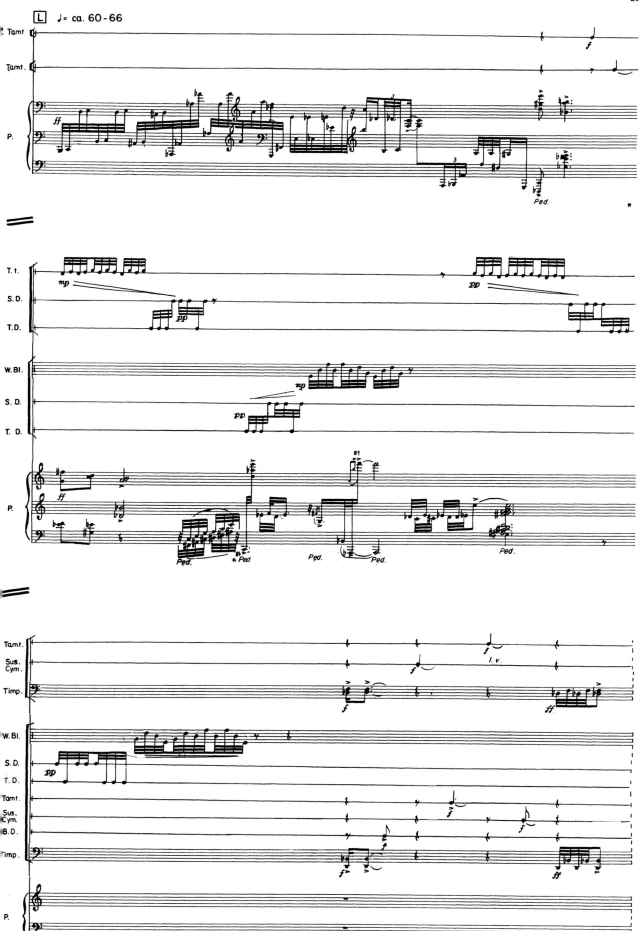

1) Play as fast as possible, legato or staccato, any pitch within the limits given

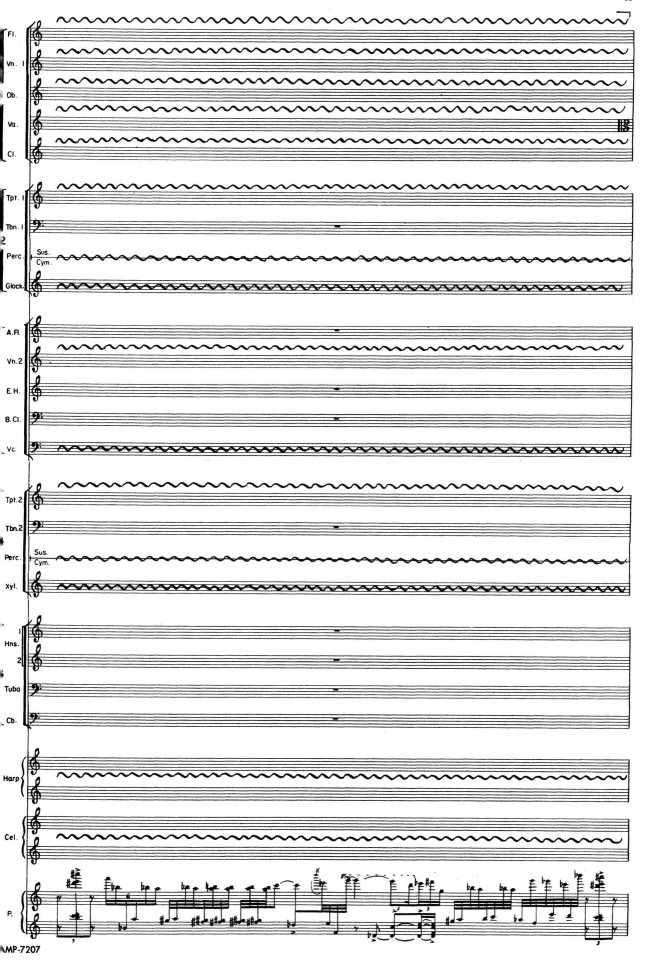

Groups I and III play at ♩ = 120, Piano at ♩ = 92. Unity between individual players and between groups and soloist is not required.

1) The squares should be played ONCE in the required order, then repeated in any order until the conductor's sign ⌐.

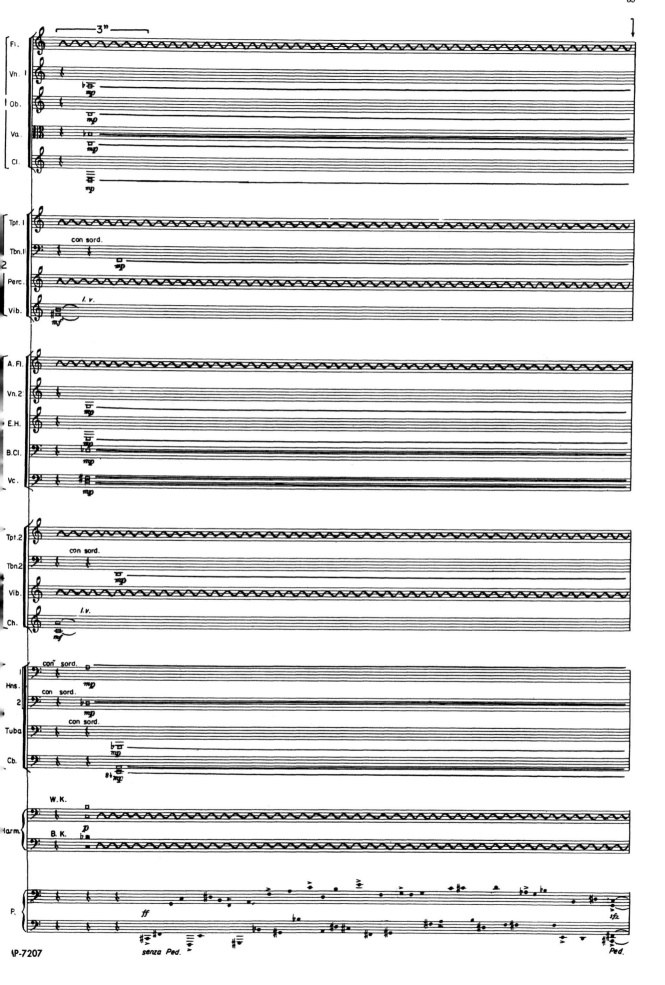

*) Breathe as necessary.

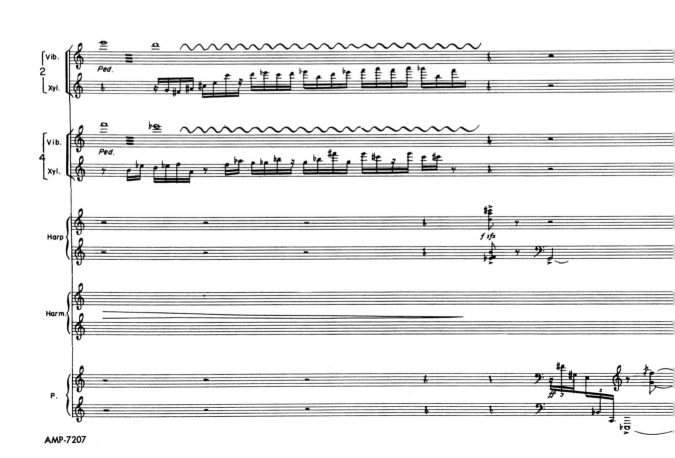

1) All instruments enter on cue, play at will the given notes (accent on D♯)
2) Conduct in 3 for Vc., Hns., Tuba, Cb <u>only.</u>

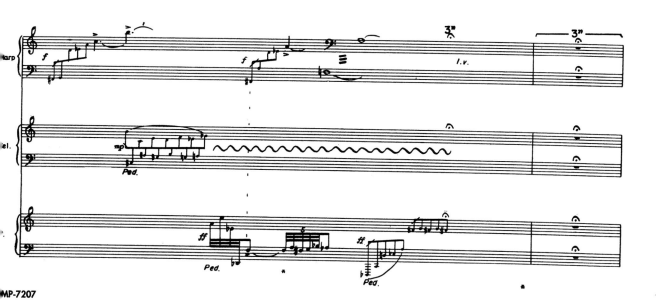

Repeat 6 to 8 times always with the same rhythm but each time a different combination of grace notes should be used after the square notes.

slow dim. to *pp*

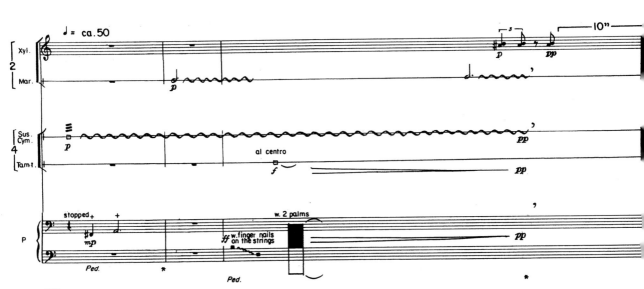